Keys to Success

TEAMWORK AND LEADERSHIP

Carol Carter
Sarah Lyman Kravits

PEARSON

Boston Columbus Indianapolis New York San Francisco Upper Saddle River
Amsterdam Cape Town Dubai London Madrid Milan Munich Paris Montreal Toronto
Delhi Mexico City Sao Paulo Sydney Hong Kong Seoul Singapore Taipei Tokyo

Editor-in-Chief: Jodi McPherson
Acquisitions Editor: Katie Mahan
Development Editor: Shannon Steed
Editorial Assistant: Clara Ciminelli
Executive Marketing Manager: Amy Judd
Senior Production Editor: Gregory Erb
Editorial Production Service: Electronic Publishing Services Inc.
Manufacturing Buyer: Megan Cochran
Electronic Composition: Jouve
Interior Design: Electronic Publishing Services Inc.
Photo Researcher: Electronic Publishing Services Inc.
Cover Designer: John Wincek
Cover Administrator: Electronic Publishing Services Inc.

Credits and acknowledgments borrowed from other sources and reproduced, with permission, in this textbook appear on the appropriate page within text. All photos © Shutterstock.

---

10 9 8 7 6 5 4 3 2 1

ISBN 10: 0-13-285024-9
ISBN 13: 978-0-13-285024-7

Teamwork and Leadership

No man is an island, entire of itself; every man is a piece of a continent.

—John Donne, English poet, 1572–1631

In this text, you'll explore answers to these questions:

STATUS CHECK

How prepared am I to be a team player?

For each statement, circle the number that best describes how often it applies to you.
1 = never 2 = seldom 3 = sometimes 4 = often 5 = always

1.	I tend toward working together rather than competing.	1 2 3 4 5
2.	I can accurately "read" people's emotions by their facial expressions, body language, and tone of voice.	1 2 3 4 5
3.	I am comfortable working with people whose personalities differ from mine.	1 2 3 4 5
4.	I am aware of my skills and talents and am comfortable offering them to others.	1 2 3 4 5
5.	I enjoy working in a group.	1 2 3 4 5
6.	I communicate my ideas clearly to others.	1 2 3 4 5
7.	I am able to motivate people toward a common goal.	1 2 3 4 5
8.	I meet deadlines and follow through on tasks.	1 2 3 4 5
9.	When I have a vision of what is possible, I convey it effectively to others.	1 2 3 4 5
10.	I act towards others as I want them to act towards me.	1 2 3 4 5

Each of the topics in these statements is covered in this text. Note those statements for which you circled a 3 or lower. Skim this text to see where those topics appear, and pay special attention to them as you read, learn, and apply new strategies.

STUDENT *Profiles*

Anna couldn't wait to start her new job at ParaTech, Inc. As a programmer, she figured she'd have plenty of time to focus on writing code, researching new technologies on the Web, attending technical conferences, and keeping her Facebook page updated. However, she did not realize how much time she would have to spend collaborating with team members and attending meetings. Suddenly her focus and drive seemed to be a liability. When she interrupted people in the meetings to get them back on track, they didn't appreciate it. When she tried to hide out in her cubicle and get some work done by herself, her manager said she wasn't a team player.

If only her manager would let her focus on her part of the project and leave her alone. Why did she have to work with the rest of the team? In fact, Anna was pretty sure that she could do a better job working by herself than working with the team. After all, that's what she did in her college coursework. She had done well because she knew how to hole up in her room, work hard, and study. She rarely made time for socializing and extracurricular activities because she found books and computer programs a lot easier to understand than people.

Yet here she was in her first professional job, realizing that working hard by herself wasn't getting her anywhere. She wondered how she was ever going to get the hang of working with a team. And she knew that if she didn't, she'd probably be out of a job.

Like Anna, no matter how hardworking, brilliant, or good at problem solving you are, you can't do it all by yourself. In today's world, projects are usually too big to be completed by one person, and problems are often too complex to be solved by one person. Instead, a team of people needs to be involved. And when people work together, personalities and communication styles come into play. In this text we look at what makes teams "tick," including working with different personality styles, gaining leadership qualities, and dealing with conflict and stress. Becoming someone who can succeed in a team setting means becoming someone who can succeed at any job.

What is a team and why are teams important?

People form groups of all types and sizes. However, not every group is a team. Consider this definition:

A **team** is a group of people working together towards a common goal.[1]

In today's world, almost everything is accomplished by teams. Large companies often use project teams that span the globe. Small companies use teams to ensure that their products and services reach their customers. Non-profit organizations put teams together to accomplish goals. Instructors teach and develop curriculum in teams, and work in teams with counselors, administrators, and other academic employees. Government workers from local to national levels work in teams. Aware of the importance of working with others, academic institutions have increased the teamwork component of many courses, and students work together both in person and online to create documents, put together presentations, and complete projects.

The prime advantage to working in teams is the ability to combine skills and talents. An academic or work team benefits from a wide array of skills that no single student or employee could possess alone, from analytical skills to marketing skills to technical skills and everything in between. Complex projects at school or in the workplace demand all of these skills, especially when things need to get done in a specific time frame.

Savvy employers look for employees who are good team players. However, working on a team is not always easy, as you can tell by the disadvantages that appear in Key 1.

Teamwork and collaboration

Collaboration is the lifeblood of any team. Even when project teams are not large or global, collaboration is essential. **Collaboration** is the act of working effectively with others to achieve a common goal. It needs to be built on trust, which can only be achieved through honesty, openness, consistency, and respect.

1. **Honesty** means that team members tell one another the truth, not just what each wants to hear. They feel comfortable disclosing problems so that other members can join in the problem-solving process and help overcome obstacles.

ADVANTAGES AND DISADVANTAGES OF TEAMWORK

ADVANTAGES	DISADVANTAGES
Generates multiple ideas for solving problems, making it easier to resolve issues.	Slows down the problem-solving process because of discussion and disagreements. This is particularly true when teams grow larger. As a result, deadlines may be compromised.
Provides wide pool of talents, letting members work together to complete tasks.	Potentially challenging for employees who prefer working alone or are not comfortable working with people with widely divergent skills and backgrounds.
Strengthens bonds between employees and improves their job satisfaction.	Allows some team members to do less work than others and not participate as much.

2. **Openness** means that team members are not afraid to say what is on their minds; they do not fear repercussions for communicating their thoughts. They share information because they are confident that people won't make fun of their ideas.
3. **Consistency** means that each team member works, and interacts, in a consistent manner. This allows members of the team to know what to expect from one another. Progress toward a goal can suffer when team members are inconsistent with their work, meeting attendance, communication, or even mood.
4. **Respect** means that team members see one another as vital parts of the team. They speak and behave respectfully toward one another. They listen to everyone's ideas without judgment, and offer constructive criticism.

To get an idea of what the four components of trust look like, consider two teams, as in Key 2. One operates on distrust and competition (Team A), and the other operates on trust and collaboration (Team B). Both teams consist of people who have never before worked together. And both teams have been tasked with coming up with a "give to get" idea that will attract more customers to buy a new cell phone product. Which team is most likely to get the job done, on time and with good quality results?

What all this means is that in a collaborative environment founded on trust, team members can stay focused, communicate more clearly, and help one another succeed, which consistently leads to better outcomes.

The idea of collaboration may take some time to get used to in a culture of competition fostered by sports, media, and business. But in the end, the benefits of collaboration almost always trump the results of a focus on competition. Alfie Cohen, a well-known author of books on human behavior and education, conducted over 400 studies to research the effects of competition on classrooms and organizations. The results? (1) Competition is not required for optimal results and (2) optimal results usually require an *absence* of competition. Cohen found that in the workplace when people started working together, rather than working against each other, productivity increased dramatically.[2]

Key 2

COMPETITION VS. **COLLABORATION**

TEAM A: COLLABORATION & TRUST	TEAM B: COMPETITION

TEAM A: COLLABORATION & TRUST

Marianne, the team leader, asks her four members to write down three things: what they are good at, what they are interested in, and what they don't like doing. She finds out that Paolo has done advertising copy editing before, and is quite good at it, but always wanted to try his hand at advertising artwork. So, she pairs him up with Tamar, who is an experienced graphics artist. Scott likes giving presentations, so he'll be conducting focus groups. Lianna is good with numbers, so Marianne asks her to work with Scott to analyze the focus group results.

All the members of the team know what they are supposed to do, and feel less stressed knowing that other people on the team will be working closely with them, helping them whenever necessary.

Chances are, the team will do a terrific job!

TEAM B: COMPETITION

William, the team leader, tells his four members what they will be doing without finding out what they like to do or what they do well. Worse, he tells the team that incompetence will not be tolerated, and any one who turns in their work late will be penalized. Finally he says, "May the best man or woman win!" William has set the scene for competition, not collaboration.

Carlos is upset he's designing the product logo and he's already burned out from doing graphics work for the last project. Janelle is anxious because she's supposed to write ad copy and she's never done that kind of writing before. Bernard is excited about leading focus groups, but he doesn't know much about what's involved, and he's embarrassed to ask anyone for assistance. Heather seems happy because she'll be analyzing the focus group results and doesn't have to get involved until the end of the project.

There's a good chance the team will never even finish this project. At the very least, the stage has been set for miscommunication, error, sub-par work, and missing deadlines.

How do you and others interact in a team?

Now that you have a sense of what a team is and what teamwork involves, it's time to look at personality types that make up a team. Start with your own personality, because an important step in the process of understanding others is to understand yourself.

Take a look at the four most common workplace personalities. These personalities also apply to working in groups on academic projects and appear in different quadrants of Key 3. Your position in a quadrant depends on your level of comfort communicating with others and on how people-oriented you are.

Descriptions of the different personality types follow. As you read them, think about which personality sounds like you. Remember, no one is ever 100 percent one personality. Each person generally has one or two quadrants in which they are most

Key 3 PERSONALITY TYPES

comfortable, but may have elements of other quadrants and can operate in other modes when necessary.

■ ***Driver.*** These individuals are action-oriented and more concerned with results than with people. In general, people who are drivers are good communicators and are adept at telling you what they want and when they want it. Conversely, they do not tend to be the best listeners. Here are some of their typical qualities.

- Decisive
- Direct
- Assertive
- Risk taker
- Competitive
- Independent
- Demanding

■ ***Analytical.*** These individuals are data-oriented and more concerned with facts than with people. In general, people who are analytical are skilled at organizing information and analyzing it in a logical manner. They are usually good with details and appreciate structure. Their communication skills are often not well-developed and they tend to have difficulty making decisions because they tend to need "more data." Here are some of their typical qualities.

- Precise
- Orderly
- Deliberate
- Cautious
- Logical
- Systematic
- Controlled

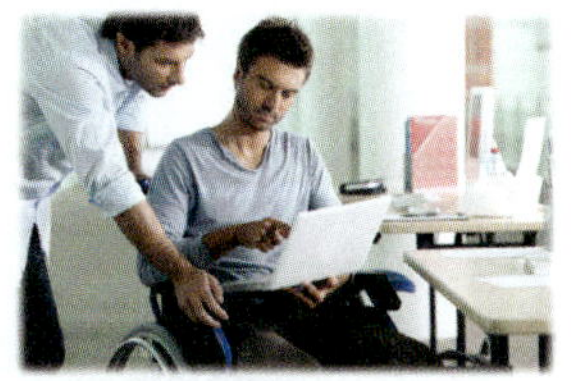

■ ***Amiable.*** These individuals are people-oriented. They are very concerned with how people get along. In general, people who are amiable are dependable, loyal, and easy-going. They do not enjoy dealing with hard facts and impersonal details, and prefer interacting with people. They are usually described as warm and sensitive, and know how to make decisions based on how they feel. Here are some of their typical qualities.

- Loyal
- Sympathetic
- Empathetic
- Supportive
- Patient
- Considerate
- Trusting

■ ***Expressive.*** These individuals are expression-oriented. They enjoy coming up with ideas and sharing them with others. They are typically very social and like helping others. They like to express themselves verbally and can be quite dramatic. Although they are good idea-generators, they are often poor at following through or making decisions. Here are some of their typical qualities.

- Verbal
- Motivating
- Enthusiastic
- Charming
- Influential
- Optimistic
- Animated

People with different work personalities bring different qualities to the team, all of which are needed. However, each personality type needs to adjust somewhat to effectively communicate with other personalities. For example, an expressive person might need to tone it down with an analytical person—present fewer ideas, speak more slowly, and go into more detail. Someone who's a driver might have to be more personable with someone who's amiable and consider feelings, not just results. Conversely, an analytical person might need to provide less detail with a results-oriented person who's a driver and an amiable person might need to be more assertive and willing to interrupt a fast-talking expressive.

Once you identify your tendencies as well as those of others on your team, you will be more able to do two crucial things:

1. **Understand communication in the context of the person.** A driver and an expressive might both be telling you the same message, but it comes across in completely different ways. With a greater understanding of how each person operates, you will be more able to interpret the message accurately.

2. **Adjust your communication style and behavior as needed to get the results you want.** If you keep your focus on your goal, you will be less likely to cling to the idea that you should be able to communicate any way that you want. One approach will work with one person but not with another. Thinking about personalities will help you choose the right approach at the right time.

Skills, talents, likes, and dislikes

To operate most effectively on a team, you need to understand what you can contribute to a team. One way to do this is to identify your skills and talents.

■ ***Talents.*** A talent is something you are born with. For example, you may be a naturally gifted artist who can draw easily or a writer who can communicate easily with words. Although practice will allow you to grow in your areas of talent, whether you practice or not, you will always demonstrate a notable level of ability.

■ ***Skills.*** A skill is something that is learned and must be practiced to remain viable. For example, you may have learned to play the piano, but get rusty when you don't practice. Or perhaps you learned a programming language in school, but haven't used it in awhile, so you need to brush up on it.

Let your teammates know what you're good at so they can keep your skills and talents in mind as decisions are made about who will take on which task. The more your teammates know about what you can contribute, the more likely they are to use your knowledge and experience, and benefit from your contributions. Likewise, if you are aware of the talents and skills of your teammates, you can use that information to make suggestions about how to divide up tasks. If you are assigned a task that is much more easily and effectively completed by another team member, for example, you can speak up and try to rearrange tasks in a more productive manner.

Keep in mind that you will not always be able to do something you are good at, or something you like to do, with a team. Ultimately the list and division of tasks will depend on the unique combination of what needs to be done, who is doing it, and when and how it needs to be done. In addition, the team leader will usually take the lead in assigning tasks, and needs to distribute them so team members are required to put in similar amounts of effort. However, having an understanding of skills and preferences will help teams and leaders make the most effective possible assignments.

Knowing what you like to do and don't like to do is also a consideration when looking at how you might contribute to a team.

■ ***Likes.*** You know what you like, whether or not you are good at it. A team may give you an opportunity to try things you're interested in and enjoy. Even if you are not highly skilled in what you are tasked to do, by pairing up with someone more skilled on the team you can gain valuable experience. Remember, if you like doing something, you're more likely to stick with it, and teams benefit from members with perseverance.

■ ***Dislikes.*** It's equally important to let your team know what you are **not** interested in. This is especially important if you don't want to do something you are good at, because teammates may assume you like doing it and assign you that duty. To avoid this, let your teammates know when you do not enjoy a particular task. That way, they may call upon you in emergencies to perform that task, but they will not ask you to do it all the time.

The more you like what you're doing, the more likely you are to keep doing it . . . and doing it well.

Emotional intelligence (EI)

Your **emotional intelligence (EI)** helps you to collaborate with others and become a better team player. Psychologists John Mayer, Peter Salovey, and David Caruso define emotional intelligence (EI) as the ability to understand "one's own and other's emotions and the ability to use this information as a guide to thinking and behavior."[3] According to this definition, it isn't enough to just *understand* what you and others feel. An emotionally intelligent person uses that understanding to choose how to *think* and how to *act*.

People with high EI can typically do the following:

1. **Accurately perceive emotions in themselves and others**. People with high EI understand emotional language and signals. They are perceptive and can easily read others by observing their facial expressions, body language, and voices. They are also self-aware and can tell when their own emotions are interfering with their communication—and can then do something about it.

2. **Manage emotions to attain specific goals**. People with high EI know how to keep calm in a crisis and help others to do the same. They know how to convey important messages with the right emotion to get buy-in from others. This makes them especially good at inspiring and motivating others. They understand how certain words and actions can impact others, and manage their behavior accordingly.

In general, people with high EI are sought after team members because they have excellent interpersonal skills. In fact, according to the Institute for Health and Human Potential, high EI contributes to improved job performance and stronger leadership skills.[4]

To help you understand EI and its value to teamwork, imagine that you are working with a team of people on a new product design. The project deadline is fast approaching and progress on the project has come to a standstill because of serious design problems. The team has been putting in 10-hour days for months, with people occasionally working weekends. Many members of the team believe that if the project fails, they will be fired. But no one knows for sure. All you know is that you are exhausted and worried.

Unbeknownst to you and the rest of the team, the manager has spoken with the client about the design issues, and the client has agreed to extend the project deadline. The manager has now called an emergency meeting with the team.

Key 4 describes two ways the manager might conduct the meeting, depending on whether he has high or low EI. You be the judge of which way is the most effective.

The low EI manager chooses the route of intimidation. He ignores (or is unaware) of his team's fatigue and anxiety. He thinks that by yelling he can get more out of them when it is likely there is not much left to give. The high EI manager recognizes what his team has gone through, acknowledges their efforts, and gives them a chance to regroup. This team is far more likely to succeed. Even if the team with the low EI manager manages to get the job done, chances are the quality of the work will be compromised because of the unproductive atmosphere the manager created.

It is important to acknowledge here that skills are crucial. For example, even a person with extraordinary emotional intelligence could not perform surgery without medical training. However, because EI is so crucial to effective communication in

Key 4

LOW EI VS. HIGH EI

MANAGER A: LOW EI	MANAGER B: HIGH EI
Your manager immediately tells everyone how disappointed he is with the team's performance and starts yelling at certain team members for their lack of progress. He berates each team member, one at a time, and picks on their individual personalities and behaviors.	Your manager looks around at the worried faces in the group and calmly says that although the project is behind, it's not the end of the world. He lets everyone know that he talked to the client and explained the problems, and the client is OK with a delay. The manager also thanks everyone for their very hard work and acknowledges their fatigue.
Then he tells everyone that they are going to have to put in longer hours and get the problem solved . . . or else. He neglects to mention the extension of the deadline because he wants to make sure everyone is "motivated."	He goes on to say that he knows the team will solve the design problem, but not when they're so exhausted. He tells everyone to take the rest of the day off and come back tomorrow with a fresh outlook. He says that from now on, people will only work 8 hours a day because 10-hour days are burning everyone out.

relationships, and team function depends on those relationships working well, it is a strong predictor of work and life success.

What is leadership?

When you think of a leader, your first thought may be of someone in a highly visible and powerful position—the president of the United States or the chancellor of Germany, the CEO of Microsoft or Ford Motor Company, the Dalai Lama or the Pope. However, there are many ways to lead, and not all leaders carry such a high profile.

Think of the community where you live. You may know of leaders such as people in local government positions, deans of educational institutions, and business owners. You probably can also think of people who you consider leaders even though they hold no official position—they just seem to motivate people, or set an example that others want to follow.

Definitions of leadership

There are two ways to define leadership:

1. The ability and process of motivating people to move toward a common goal
2. The ability and process of affecting thoughts and behaviors of others[5]

The first definition refers to a more visible, typical kind of leadership. It is the job of the CEO of a company, for example, to motivate people employed by the company to create and sell the company's products; likewise, it is the job of a quarterback to motivate his team to move the ball downfield. However, any person—whether a CEO, a quarterback, or anyone else—can also lead in the second way, by setting an example that inspires others to positive thought and productive action. This second type of leader may or may not have a typical leadership position, but an official position is not necessary to lead by example.

Think of leaders who have inspired you. Do you look up to humanitarian heroes such as Mother Theresa or Nelson Mandela? Perhaps you admire agents of social change such as Martin Luther King, Jr., or Gloria Steinem. Maybe you are motivated by

KNOW IT

What's Your EI?

Think about Emotional Intelligence (EI) and its importance in the workplace, especially on teams. Perhaps you consider yourself quite intuitive when it comes to "reading" others, or maybe you find the emotions of others a mystery. The Greater Good Science Center at the University of California developed a photo quiz that you can take online to discover more about how well you read emotions on the faces of others. You may be surprised by the results! Take the Online Quiz at http://greatergood.berkeley.edu/ei_quiz/

WHAT'S YOUR TYPE?

Draw a star in a location on the personality quadrant that represents your "comfort" zone—the place where you typically operate when working with others. Then answer the following questions on paper or in an electronic file.

1. What behaviors or feelings do you typically exhibit that made you decide to put the dot in that location?
2. When you get highly stressed, do you feel you stay in the same quadrant? If not, where do you "go?"

the leadership of influential politicians, writers, scientists, inventors, and businesspeople. Consider whether these people embody just one or both of the definitions of leadership. The most powerful leaders usually emerge from a recipe consisting of both.

Components of leadership

There are several factors, or components, that make up the experience of leadership. They are as follows:[6]

1. **1.** Leadership is a process, not a state of being. A leader can't just be a leader when given a title—a leader does. Leadership demands action, following a process toward a goal.
2. Leadership means influencing the thoughts, feelings, and actions of others, whether by example or by directive (see Key 5 for the ways that effective leaders set an example).
3. Leadership happens in the context of a group. A leader working alone is not a leader—there must be followers involved.
4. Leadership involves reaching a goal together with efforts from others in the group.
5. Leadership demands that the group and the leader share the same goal.

These components show that leadership extends far beyond the leader, even though the attention often goes to the leader alone. A leader is able to generate motion and energy, moving currents of action and communication throughout a group and propelling them toward a common goal. Leaders of any scope, from the head of the United Nations to the chairperson of a community board, get things done.

Being a leader now

Leadership is not just for graduates who have embarked on careers. Students can and should find opportunities to lead, either by action or by example. Leadership is important for students for two reasons—one, to make things happen inside and outside of your academic community while you are working toward a degree, and two, to build leadership skills that will serve you later in the workplace and in life.

What can you do now to be a leader and build leadership skills?

▶ **Help to lead organizations that interest you.** Once you have joined an organization and learned more about how it works, consider pursuing a leadership position in the club. Find out more about what these positions involve (duties, time commitment) and see what might suit you best.

▶ **Form study groups.** Take the lead on getting fellow students together in person or online for a study group. When the group is formed, take a turn leading a meeting, or come up with a plan for preparing for a test.

▶ **Express yourself in front of others.** When an opportunity to speak in front of others comes up, take it. Present in front of a class, post a message to your class online, or speak to members of a club at a meeting.

▶ **Volunteer in or outside your academic community.** Making a difference for others around you can build leadership skills on its own. If you have a strong

EFFECTIVE LEADERS SET **AN EXAMPLE THROUGH...**

BEHAVIOR	FOLLOW-THROUGH	POSITIVE SELF-IDENTITY	VALUES	VISION
Leaders model most effective, positive behaviors. When they ask others to behave in a certain way, they do the same. They take responsibility for their actions.	Leaders do what they say they will do. They meet deadlines and deliver on their promises.	Leaders are aware of both their strengths and weaknesses. They believe in themselves and work to grow and improve.	Leaders demonstrate values that inspire team members as well as support team goals.	Leaders have a vision of what is possible and know how to convey it. They maintain their vision in the face of obstacles.

interest in an organization, you may even consider pursuing a specific leadership position with the organization, or heading up a particular project.

▶ **Take initiative at work.** Speak out respectfully about systems, teams, or situations that aren't working well and need to be adjusted. Talk to a supervisor about ideas you have that you might be able to implement. Set an example for others with whom you work.

▶ **Start a club.** If you have a particular interest and don't see a group that focuses on that interest, why not start one yourself? Communicate with other students at your institution to see who else might be interested. Have an initial conversation or meeting and come up with some specific goals. If your group takes root, see if your institution will recognize it as an official club.

▶ **Tutor or mentor others.** Helping other students with academic development, career planning, or personal needs builds all kinds of leadership skills.

In the next section on how teams operate, you will read more specific strategies for how to lead a team.

How can a team operate effectively?

When a group of people come together to work on a project, it takes time for the group to become a team. During that time, the group goes through several phases.

- **Forming.** This is the chaotic stage where members of the team get to know one another, figure out their strengths, and determine a direction for the team.
- **Storming.** This is the uncomfortable stage where conflicts arise because people begin to show their "real" selves to one another. Disagreements and conflict can derail team progress, which is why people must keep communicating during this stage.
- **Norming.** This is the comfortable stage where the group recommits, accepts its roles and responsibilities, and begins to build consensus.
- **Performing.** This is the dynamic stage where the team actually accomplishes things. Now that members have a good understanding of their strengths and weaknesses, they can better divide up the tasks and get work done on a project.

- **Adjourning.** This is the final stage when the team finishes its project. During this stage, members discuss what went well, what could have been done better, and then the team dissolves . . . or gets ready for another project!

Even if your team doesn't march through these stages in this exact way, knowing about them will help you understand what's happening on your team and make choices that help move things along. For example, if a conflict arises and you realize it is a typical sign of the "storming" stage, you may be more able to stay calm and keep the lines of communication open.

Standard guidelines

For a team to accomplish a goal, it's a good idea to follow some established guidelines. Here are some that every team should follow.

1. Before anything else, **identify the desired goal** so the team starts working with the end in mind.
2. Once team members know the goal, **define roles and expectations**. Who is going to do what and how well does it need to be done? If team members are clear about communicating their skills and talents, the team leader should be able to delegate various tasks.
3. Then it's time for **planning and scheduling**. Just because the team members know what they are supposed to do, it doesn't mean they know *when* they are supposed to do it. Certain tasks may depend on others, so the team leader needs to figure out a realistic schedule.
4. Throughout the process, the team must **monitor its performance** to see if deadlines are being met and teammates are performing their tasks to the best of their abilities.
5. Finally, the team needs to **evaluate its performance**. What went well? What didn't? What might team members change next time—either with this same team or another? Make sure you don't skip this crucial opportunity to learn from the experience and improve on it.

Leading and participating

A team member and a team leader have things in common. Both work on a team to ensure its success, and both share a common goal. The primary difference between a team player and team leader is that the **team player** is responsible for his or her contributions to the team, while the **team leader** is responsible for his or her contributions as well as the success of the entire team.

Tips for Participation

Remember, every team leader is also a team member. Team members need the following qualities to be effective on the team:

- Be clear on your skills and talents so you know how to best contribute.
- Listen well to others without interrupting or thinking about what to say next.
- Concentrate on the task at hand, rather than worrying about other things.
- Take notes so that you do not forget what is said.
- Communicate clearly so your team understands what you are trying to say. This is particularly important when you are giving instructions or documenting something that happened.
- Set goals for yourself so that you know what to do and when.
- Manage your own time so that you complete tasks on time.
- Follow through—finish what you start.

Tips for Team Leadership

If you are a team leader, you will need particular strategies to effectively lead your team. The first set of strategies comes directly from the components of leadership:

1. Because leadership is a process, the leader must keep the process moving. Create and update agendas, communicate regularly, address problems before they fester, motivate toward deadlines.
2. Because leadership means influencing others, the leader must choose actions and attitudes with care. Do what you want others to do, and act as you want others to act.
3. Because leadership happens in the context of a group, the leader has to remember that he or she cannot accomplish the goal without the team members. Be careful not to value yourself over others.
4. Because leadership involves reaching a goal together, the leader has to delegate. Avoid thinking you can do everything and taking on too many tasks—parcel them out so that everyone is helping the ball move forward.
5. Because leadership demands a common goal, the leader has to make sure everyone is on the same page. Do this at the first meeting and clarify periodically if you need to.

Here are some additional important tips for effective leadership.

- Communicate your vision clearly so that your team understands and believes it. If you are able to convey what your vision will accomplish, you will be more likely to inspire others to share the vision so that they want to work together to make it a reality. Telling a story or describing a scenario can help make the vision seem real.
- Motivate your team members as they work toward the goal. This often involves repeatedly reminding team members of the benefits of the achieving the goal and complimenting them on their contributions.
- Set goals for the team so they know what you want them to do—both group goals and goals for individual team members.
- Organize so that each team member knows what he or she is responsible for. Once you have delegated tasks, set up a system to communicate progress.
- Create schedules so that the team knows what must be completed and when. Monitor schedules and adjust if necessary. Emphasize that team members must communicate with you if they are falling behind or will have trouble making a deadline.

NOTE: Even if you are not the team leader, you can still use these leadership skills to produce results.

What strategies help teams achieve their goals?

Moving through these stages and following these guidelines requires focus, motivation, and some specific success strategies. Each of the following strategies helps teams to achieve their goals successfully.

Put goals, tasks, and schedules in writing

Team goals and individual tasks and responsibilities need to be in writing. A good time to draw up a written record of what the team aims to do and what each team member is assigned to contribute is at the end of, or after, the first meeting. Have one team member take notes during that meeting and then distribute a document that outlines the main goal, breaks down the tasks, and shows who is supposed to complete what, indicating due dates and other scheduling items. Other team members should then have the opportunity to comment on the document in case there are any misunderstandings that need to be cleared up.

Team meetings allow team members to share how things are going and identify any issues that need resolving. For meetings to be effective, an **agenda** is a necessity.

An agenda is simply a written list of goals you want to accomplish during the meeting, in the order you want to accomplish them. The benefit of an agenda is that it keeps people on topic and prevents "scope creep." Scope creep is what happens when people go off on tangents during the meeting, talking about unrelated items, or they go into far too much detail for the rest of the team. The result is a derailed meeting that tries to cover too much information and only accomplishes frustration.

An agenda does not ensure that the meeting goes exactly as planned, but it certainly helps keep things on track. A typical agenda, such as that in Key 6, usually consists of these parts:

1. **Purpose.** Why are you holding the meeting?
2. **Goal.** When the meeting is over, what do you hope to accomplish?

SAMPLE
AGENDA

Date:	July 7, 2011
Time:	10:00 AM - 2:30 PM (with lunch break)
Location:	Calypso Room
Invitees:	All members of the training team.
Goal:	Develop rough outline for new training booklet.
Preparation:	Please bring paper and pencil, along with any thoughts about the new training booklet.

Time	Meeting Task
10:00–10:15	Quick introduction to project
10:15–10:30	Identify audience for booklet (job title, background, frustrations, motivations)
10:30–10:45	Identify job tasks audience must be able to perform
10:45–11:00	Use 80–20 rule to select the tasks we want to cover in the booklet (80 percent of the time, our audience will be performing 20 percent of the job tasks — we want to cover that 20 percent)
1:00 - 11:15	BREAK
11:15 — 11:45	Brainstorm topics to address those tasks
11:45 — 12:15	Organize the topics into a rough outline
12:15 — 1:15	LUNCH
1:15 — 1:30	Identify locations for activities in the outline
1:30 — 2:00	Create one-paragraph descriptions for each activity
2:00 —2:15	Select "sample" topics from the outline and assign one person to each topic
2:15 — 2:30	Set up date for next meeting to find out what it's like to work on a topic (what's hard and what's easy) and create a schedule

3. **Expectations.** What do you expect people to bring to the meeting? To contribute?
4. **Logistics.** When and where are you holding the meeting, and how long will it be? Include instructions for attending remotely if you are meeting by conference call or Internet.

Follow meeting etiquette

Even if you follow an agenda, you still have to manage the meeting and the people in it to produce the best results. This is where meeting etiquette comes into play.

▶ **Show up on time.** It's disruptive to arrive after the meeting starts. If you cannot avoid being late, call, text, or e-mail to let people know. Then apologize briefly when you arrive.

▶ **Be prepared.** Make sure you have all necessary materials. Always do a "tech check" ahead of time to make sure your equipment is working (computer, software, and video projector).

▶ **Don't interrupt.** This is difficult for most people to do. However, when it's your turn, you will appreciate not being interrupted. A teammate who listens is one who is respected.

▶ **Use polite language.** No matter how angry or frustrated you feel, do not get overly emotional and let your words and actions convey extreme emotion. The minute you shout or swear, you lose your credibility. Always speak the way you would like to be spoken to.

▶ **Respect confidentiality.** If someone says something in the meeting that needs to stay confidential, do not discuss it when you leave the meeting; otherwise, people will no longer trust you.

▶ **Discuss issues in person.** If you have an issue with someone on the team, do not complain about the individual in front of the rest of the team. Instead, talk to him or her privately, after the meeting. Why? Because when you get angry with a teammate in front of the rest of the team, your teammates naturally assume you will do the same to them. As a result, they are less likely to participate or offer ideas in the future.

▶ **Acknowledge teammates.** Give credit where credit is due. Acknowledge the contributions of others, even if you did most of the work.

▶ **Avoid interruptive technology.** Do not send text messages, e-mails, instant messages or take phone calls during a meeting. It is essential to give your full attention to the meeting and your teammates, without distractions. Otherwise, people consider you rude and assume you do are not taking the meeting seriously. Additionally, you will be less likely to remember important aspects of the meeting. Some companies are even requiring that meeting attendees drop their cell phones and PDAs in a box before they sit down to a meeting.

Make decisions effectively

All teams must make decisions in order to achieve their goals. Key 7 shows you four common decision-making models. Your team may use several of these models, depending on the situation.

▶ **Authoritarian.** The team leader makes the decision. This type of decision-making model is useful in emergency situations, but generally is not acceptable because team members will feel dictated to.

▶ **Group Deciders.** A small group from the team makes the decision. This is better than having only one person make the decision, but most team members will still feel left out of the decision-making process.

▶ **Majority Rules.** Team members vote on the issue and the position with the majority of votes wins. **NOTE:** The team must decide ahead of time what a "majority" is: more than half? Two-thirds? This process may still leave a few members feeling their opinions have not been heard.

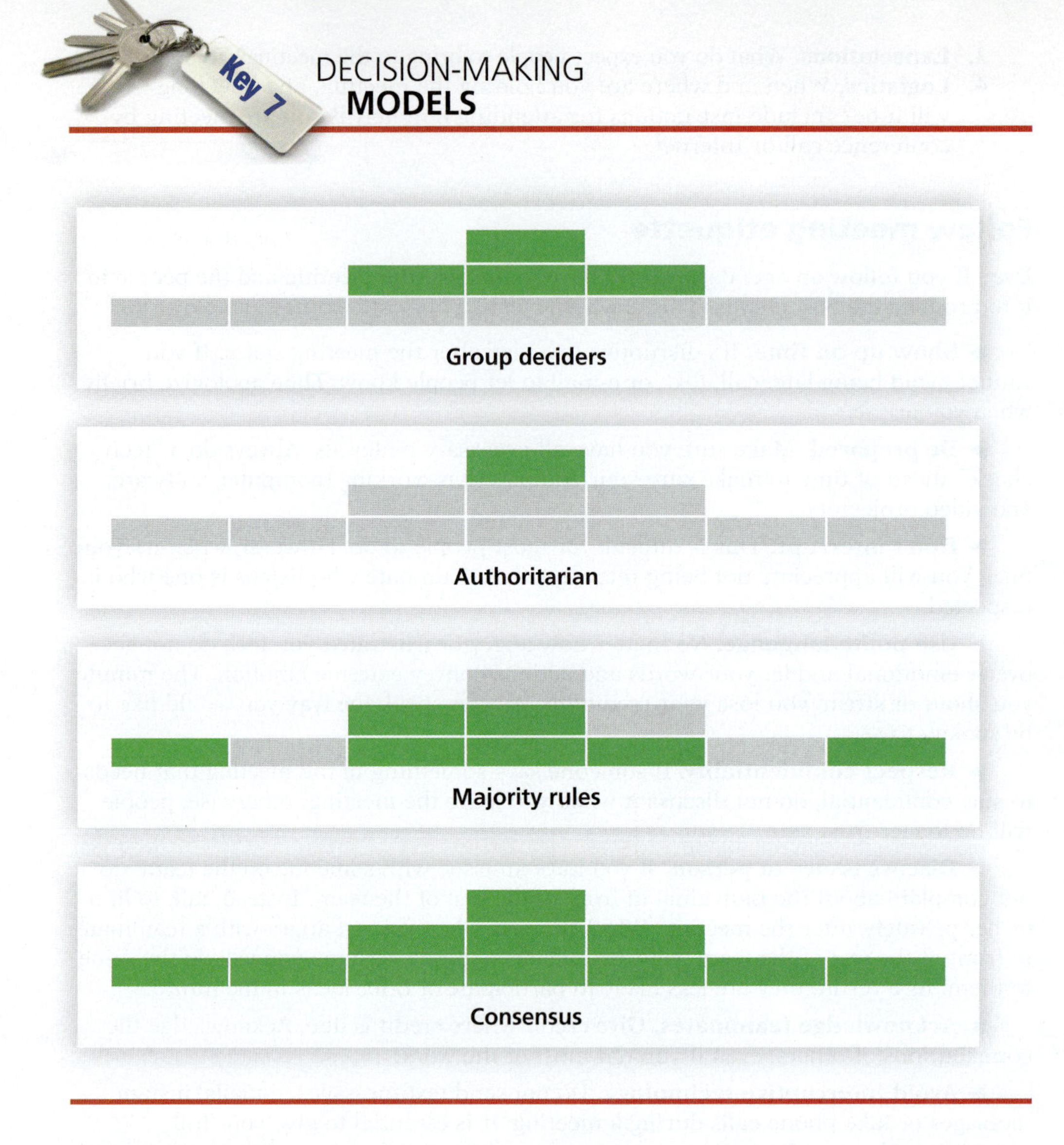

▶ **Consensus.** All team members express their position. They must then come to a unanimous decision by agreeing or choosing to abstain. This takes a long time (not good for emergencies), but results in a decision that everyone can live with.

You may find that your team is more comfortable with one type of decision-making model. However, it's a good idea to try them all in different situations.

Be aware of detrimental roles

Even the best team can be sabotaged by team members who play roles that are detrimental to team function and goal achievement. Keep an eye out for the behaviors described in Key 8, both in others as well as yourself. If you are on a team with someone playing one of these roles, choose actions that make the best of the situation. If you find you are playing a role yourself, work to adjust your behavior so that you can help rather than hinder your team's progress.

Avoid groupthink

Even if you and your team members manage to avoid the detrimental behaviors we just described, you may still fall into the trap of "**groupthink**." This is a phenomena where members of a team begin to tacitly agree with each other's ideas to avoid

Key 8

DETRIMENTAL ROLES

DETRIMENTAL ROLE TYPE	CHARACTERISTICS OF ROLE
Lone Ranger	People who play the Lone Ranger role tend to have introverted, highly competitive personalities, and prefer to work alone because they think others slow them down. They often overwhelm the rest of the team with their intelligence and fast pace. If you happen to have lone-ranger tendencies, slow down and be patient. Work with your team so that all members feel they are contributing, rather than just you.
Know-It-All	People who play the Know-It-All role believe they know everything and close their minds to new ideas, dismissing ideas from their teammates. Often, teammates stop sharing ideas for fear of rejection, and then begin to ignore the person who seems to know it all. If you have Know-It-All tendencies, try listening to others without judging them. More importantly, consider the fact that you don't know everything and there's always something new you could learn.
Passive Aggressive	People who play the Passive Aggressive role have difficulty clearly communicating their needs. Instead of asking for what they want or honestly disagreeing with others, they say nothing. Their frustration and resentment builds, and finally they resort to withholding information or trying to "hurt" other members of the team as a way to get revenge. If this sounds like you, work on being direct in your communication. Confront the issue; don't run away from it. People can't solve a problem they don't know about, so gather up your courage and state your point of view.
The Intimidated	People who play the role of the Intimidated often have low self-esteem and imagine that everyone else on the team is smarter or more talented than they are. As a result, they give up their power and rarely share ideas because they think they are inadequate. If you have these tendencies, remind yourself of your strengths and dismiss the habitual thoughts that you are "less than" another person. You will be most effective if you can be strong and humble at the same time.
The Gossip	People who play the role of the Gossip often feel insecure or intimidated by others. They use gossiping as a way to criticize others and feel better about themselves. If you find yourself gossiping about others, consider your own strengths and let go of the tendency to criticize others. As you do, people will begin to respect you and you will respect them as well.
The Taker	People who play the role of the Taker often take credit for the work of others instead of acknowledging their efforts. Why? Because they feel insecure about their own efforts. If you notice this pattern in yourself, start acknowledging the contributions of other people, no matter how small, on a daily basis. The next time an opportunity comes up to "steal" the credit, remain silent, and see what happens!
The Slacker	People who play the role of the Slacker never volunteer and do the minimum work required of them. Individuals often behave this way because deep down, they don't believe in themselves or their abilities, and do not want to fail. If you have these tendencies, consider taking on more responsibility so that you can experience what it's like to contribute and be acknowledged for your efforts, whether they are great or small. Your teammates will begin to see you in a new light.

DETRIMENTAL ROLES (continued)

DETRIMENTAL ROLE TYPE	CHARACTERISTICS OF ROLE
Seat Filler 	Someone playing the role of the Seat Filler does nothing—even less than someone playing the Slacker role. If you find yourself in this role, you need to ask what you are afraid of and what will happen if you continue to do nothing. You may need help from a counselor, a coach, or a mental health professional, to move beyond your self-doubt and fear of failing, and break out of your self-limiting thoughts and patterns.

conflict—even when they actually object to those ideas. In other words, people pretend to agree, even when they disagree, and everyone appears to think alike.

This type of behavior is dangerous because new ideas are no longer presented and considered, team members fail to think critically about situations, and people go along with things by default. The dangers of groupthink can be seen in the failings of both the automobile industry and the financial industry. A few people noticed the industries heading for trouble and voiced their concerns. But most people simply went along with decisions that were made, and negative outcomes resulted.

A team needs to be able to communicate honestly and be open to diverse ideas, which often means managing dissent. Sometimes the most surprising and effective results come from deep and challenging disagreements among team members.

Handle conflict

If your team manages to avoid the dangers of groupthink, you are bound to run into conflict—it's a normal part of any team's process. With different types of personalities on the team, disagreement is bound to occur, but disagreement is what brings new ideas to the floor. So, rather than fear conflict, overreact to it, or escalate it, try the following steps.

1. **Determine what the issue is.** Is it a conflict of interest? A lack of role clarity? A lack of resources? A personality conflict? Once you are clear on the conflict, continue.

SPEAK IT

MEETING IN PERSON

In-person meetings give you a chance to read body language, practice good meeting etiquette, and learn to make decisions. Think of a situation where you need to set up a meeting with one or more people and come to a decision at the end.

1. Develop an agenda and distribute it to meeting attendees before the meeting.
2. Hold the meeting. Make sure to identify the goal of the meeting, observe people's body language, practice following good meeting etiquette, and try to stay on time.
3. What seemed to be most difficult about running the meeting?
4. What "rules" of etiquette got broken most often?
5. What did you notice about how people felt during the meeting when you watched their body language?
6. What type of decision–making model did you use in the meeting? Why?
7. What can you do in the future to make your meetings even more effective?

MEETING REMOTELY

You can't always meet in person when teammates are busy or live out of town. Try holding another meeting by phone with one or more people.

1. Develop an agenda and distribute it to meeting attendees before the meeting.
2. Hold the meeting. Make sure to identify the goal of the meeting, speak clearly, ask questions to make sure people hear and understand you, practice following good meeting etiquette and tips for remote meetings, and try to stay on time.
3. How was this meeting different from the live meeting?
4. What seemed to be most difficult about running the meeting?
5. What "rules" of etiquette got broken most often?
6. What did you notice about how people participated on the phone?
7. What type of decision-making model did you use in the meeting? Why?
8. What can you do in the future to make your phone meetings even more effective?

2. **Separate emotion from the message.** This means avoiding responding to the emotion in your team member's voice. Instead, listen to the message behind the emotion. What is the concern? Try to listen without judging.
3. **Respond to the group, not the individual.** When someone attacks you or argues with you, take a deep breath and do not respond immediately. Then, once you feel more centered, respond to the entire group. You can still make eye contact with the individual, but make sure to talk to the rest of the group as well. This way, the conflict does not become a personal argument.
4. **Take it offline.** If resolution is not possible during the meeting, ask to take the discussion offline and privately discuss the issue with the individual at another time, outside of the meeting.

A key tool in managing conflict is the ability to handle criticism productively.

Give and take effective criticism

Criticism is a reality in every aspect of life. Students receive it from instructors and advisors; employees receive it from supervisors and other employees; people receive it from parents, friends, partners, children, and other family members. And, of course, people criticize themselves, often excessively.

The secret to benefiting from criticism is your attitude. If you perceive all criticism as negative and damaging, or take it too personally rather than focusing on the specifics of what is being criticized, you are likely to shut down and dismiss it. The result? You don't have the opportunity to benefit from what is helpful in the criticism. However, if you work to stay open to criticism, looking carefully at the ideas for improvement within it and keeping focused on the action or behavior that is being criticized rather than taking it to heart, you may gain important insights that will help you grow and develop.

Criticism can be either **constructive** or **unconstructive**. Constructive criticism is a practical problem-solving strategy, consisting of goodwill suggestions that promote improvement or development. In contrast, unconstructive criticism focuses on what went wrong and doesn't offer alternatives that might help solve the problem. Furthermore, it is often delivered negatively, and this has even more potential to create bad feelings and shut down communication.

When offered constructively, criticism can help bring about important changes. Consider this situation: A study group member has continually been late to scheduled study sessions. Which comment from the group leader would bring about positive change? Think about it this way: Which comment would encourage you to change *your* behavior if you were the person being spoken to?

- **Constructive.** The group leader talks privately in person or over e-mail with the student: "I've noticed that you've been late a lot. We count on you to contribute. Is there a problem that is keeping you from being on time? Can we help?"
- **Unconstructive.** After the student makes yet another late arrival to the session, the leader says or types in front of everyone, "If you can't start getting here on time, there's really no point in your coming."

At school, criticism from your instructors can help you improve classwork, create higher quality papers, and do better on exams. On the job, criticism from supervisors, coworkers, or customers can help you function more effectively in whatever tasks your job involves, as well as communicate more effectively with those around you. If you remember that most people want you to succeed, you may be more able to take in the criticism and put it to productive use.

DID YOU *know...*

Teamwork is number 3 in the top 10 skills employers look for in an interview situation.[7]

Even if you think someone *doesn't* want you to succeed, consider: Why not take something useful out of a bad situation? Do whatever you can to benefit, especially if criticism is coming from a source that you cannot avoid (a supervisor on a job you want to keep for as long as possible, a family member).

Following are some pointers for both sides of the exchange—the person offering criticism as well as the person receiving it.

■ ***Offering Constructive Criticism.*** Use the following strategies to present your case effectively when you are the one with something to say:

▶ **Criticize the behavior, not the person.** Work to avoid personal attacks. "You've been late turning in your materials for the last two projects," is better than, "You're lazy," or, "You're dragging us down."

▶ **Define the specific problem.** Try to focus on the facts, backing them up with specific examples and minimizing emotions. For example: "For this project, you were assigned to turn in the research by May 12, and you didn't get it to the group until May 19. For the previous project, you were over two weeks late. Both times this prevented the group from making the deadline and it had sales consequences for the company."

▶ **Suggest new approaches and offer help.** Talk about practical ways to handle the situation. Brainstorm creative options. Help the person feel supported. How about: "What can we do to help you stay on track? Do you want to set up interim deadlines for parts of your research? Do you want one of us to send you a text or e-mail at particular intervals to remind you of the deadlines? Also, let us know if there is some problem on your end that you haven't told us about. We're here for you."

▶ **Use a positive approach and hopeful language.** Express your belief that the person can turn the situation around. "We value your input, that's why you are on this team. We know that there is a better way to work that helps you deliver on time and benefits everyone. We will brainstorm with you anytime about ways to solve this."

A positive team experience promotes a sense of unity, motivating people to cooperate more effectively and increasing productivity.[8]

■ ***Receiving Criticism.*** When you are on criticism's receiving end, try the following techniques:

▶ **Summarize the criticism.** The goal is for all to understand the situation. Listen carefully, and repeat back the information to make sure you heard accurately. The team member who turned in late work in the previous example could say: "So what we're talking about here is my turning in research late on the last two projects."

▶ **Focus on what is useful.** Try to let unconstructive comments go without responding.

▶ **Analyze the comments.** Next, evaluate what you heard. What does it mean? What is the intent? For example, the team member might consider that the person offering criticism is focused on improving the team's productiveness as a whole. If the members of the team get along well, members may also want to improve team communication and cooperation, hoping that the team will continue to be allowed to work together.

▶ **Ask for suggestions on how to change your behavior.** Be open to what others say, and think through the pros and cons of the suggestions you receive. For example, "I hear your ideas about communication and about deadlines. Perhaps we can put those ideas together. I don't think that alone either one would be enough. I've

been too overloaded with other work tasks over the last couple of months because of one of my co-workers being out on medical leave."

▶ **Come up with a plan.** Once you analyze the problem and brainstorm ways to change, choose a strategy that you and the person offering criticism both think might work. For example, "Let's set up a system where someone e-mails me with two weeks to go, ten days to go, one week to go, and four days to go—and I have to respond each time telling them where I'm at with my progress."

Manage stress

Like conflict, stress is inevitable in any team. **Stress** is the physical, mental, or emotional strain or tension you or the team feels in response to external situations that arise. For example, suppose the Vice President of the company visits your team and says you are doing a great job, but also tells you that the team must get the product out three months earlier. You might react to this news by feeling anxious and overwhelmed. Or you might feel angry. You might even feel like giving up because you have no ideas how you are going to accomplish what the Vice President wants. All of these are stress reactions.

Although you cannot always control the situations around you, you can control your reaction to them. Key 9 lists some useful tips for dealing with stress.

Make the most of virtual teamwork

A "team meeting" used to refer to a group of people coming together in the same room. However, modern technology has made it possible for people not working in the same geographic location to hold meetings. Teams who work remotely, by phone, e-mail, instant messaging, conference call, or web conference are referred to as **virtual teams**. Students taking online courses work almost exclusively on virtual teams when cooperating on any project.

All of the strategies for team success that you've just read apply to any kind of team, whether virtual or in-person. In addition, here are some specific strategies for virtual team members.

■ ***Make a personal connection.*** In a virtual team, you may be unable to see another team member or meet with him or her in person. Before or after the

STRESS MANAGEMENT TECHNIQUES

STRESS MANAGEMENT TECHNIQUE	ACTIONS TO TAKE
Change your state	Change your physical state and you can change your state of mind. If you are sitting, try standing or walking. If you are standing, sit down and relax. If you are talking, try being silent.
Take a break	Take time to get away from your current work environment. Take a short walk, even if it's inside the building. Take a stretch break to get your blood flow going. Do some deep breathing to calm yourself.
Create a system of balance	Pay attention to your body and know when it's time for a break. Is your neck sore and your shoulders tight? Is your breathing shallow? Do you feel irritated, angry, or overwhelmed? It's time for a break! Learn to balance periods of hard work with real breaks.
Know when it's time to refuel	Refueling involves more than just a short break. This means taking time out to eat, rest, breathe deeply, exercise, talk to others, or sit by yourself without any interruptions. All work and no play makes you a stressed out person!

WRITE IT

HANDLING CONFLICT

Think of a time when where you had a conflict with someone in a group setting and the situation did not go well.

1. Write down what happened.

2. Looking back, think about what you could have done differently. Now write an alternative version of the situation, using the knowledge you have about what causes conflict and how to handle it.

MANAGING STRESS

People react to stressful situations in different ways—learning to recognize and change those behaviors is the first step to managing stress.

1. Write down a list of things that tend to stress you.

2. Write down your typical responses to stress.

3. Based on what you've learned, write down alternative responses that you might try.

meeting, contact the person by phone or e-mail to introduce yourself and share some personal information so the individual knows something about you.

- ***Choose the right communication tool.*** Videoconferences are good for large groups who need to see one another and conference calls are good for small to medium groups that need to hear one another. Groupware, like Net Meeting, is good for groups that need to view information on the computer screen while they discuss things on the phone and collaborative writing software, like Google Docs, is good for groups that need to work together to write and edit documents. Finally, webcasts are good for groups where one leader needs to make a presentation on the Internet to a large number of people.

Teamwork is found frequently in the animal kingdom. For example, birds called oxpeckers ride the backs of rhinos and eat ticks and other insects that live there. As with human teamwork, everybody benefits: The oxpeckers get food, and the rhino gets rid of parasites.[9]

- ***Speak clearly.*** During conference calls, people from other parts of the country, or from other countries, may be listening. To make sure that your accent or language does not get in the way, speak clearly and more slowly than usual. Always ask if your listeners can hear you, and adjust your volume accordingly.

- ***Take turns.*** As good as the technology may be, a consistent problem with phone or web meetings is that people tend to talk over one another. When two people are speaking at the same time, often neither can be understood. Additionally, you may experience a delay in hearing or seeing a virtual team member, depending on how strong the phone or web connection is. Make sure you let team members finish a point before you chime in. You may even want to come up with a way to indicate, visually or verbally, that a team member has something to say, and have the leader acknowledge members when it is their turn to speak.

- ***Pick up the phone.*** If you did not understand something during a conference call, try writing and e-mail and asking for clarification. If you still cannot resolve an issue, pick up the phone and make a call. E-mails can be cold and unfriendly and sometimes unclear. But hearing a voice over the phone makes things more personal and usually clears up misunderstandings.

Think back

Take action that will help you remember what you've read about teamwork and leadership. Revisit the major ideas you encountered in the text as follows:

1. Review the learning objective questions asked at the beginning of the text and write a short answer for each.
2. Go back to the **Status Check** self-assessment at the beginning of the text. Choose one item from the list that you want to develop further.
3. Set a specific goal about how to develop that item, based on what you read in this text. Describe the goal and how you plan to achieve it in a short paragraph, including a time frame and specific steps.

DO IT

This is your chance to tie together everything you've learned in the text and put your knowledge to use in the real world.

Accommodating Different Personality Types

Return to the "Know It" activity to see how you identified your own personality type (p. **11**). This time, you will explore other peoples' types as well. For the purposes of this exercise, think about either an academic group (fellow students and an instructor from a course you've taken) or a workplace group (co-workers and a manager from a job you have now or have had in the past).

1. Put a star in the location that identifies your personality type.
2. Now put a square in the location that identifies your instructor or manager's type.
3. Put triangles in the location that identifies the personality type of two fellow students or co-workers.

Note where the symbols are: are they in the same quadrant as you, or elsewhere? Are they spread out, or concentrated in one or two quadrants? Answer the following questions:

1. Think back to your experience with this group: how well did you work and communicate with each of these people in the group setting?

2. Based on your experience and how you have evaluated their types, what can you conclude about how your type generally interacts with other types?
3. What changes could you make in your own behavior to more effectively communicate with the other personality types?
4. If you were to work with this group again, what is one specific way you would communicate differently to improve your experience or outcome?

Knowing Yourself as a Team Member

As you read in the text, effective teamwork depends on team members knowing themselves well and contributing in ways that best suit them. To complete the following items, think about past experiences with study groups and/or work teams.

1. List what you consider to be your talents (abilities you were born with).
2. List what you consider to be your skills (abilities you have learned and continue to maintain).
3. List your teamwork "likes"—what you like to do when working with others.
4. List your teamwork "dislikes"—what you do **not** like to do when working with others.
5. Consider the list of detrimental behaviors (Lone Ranger, Gossip, Passive Aggressive, etc.) on p. 19.
   a. Do you exhibit any of those behaviors yourself? If so, which?
   b. Identify a specific change you can make to move away from any detrimental behavior you exhibit.
   c. Choose a behavior you have encountered in others and describe how to work with the behavior effectively in a team situation.

Taking the Lead

Resolve to put your leadership skills to use in the next six months.

1. Describe a situation in your life—personal, academic, or workplace—where you could take a leadership role.
2. Keeping in mind the components of leadership from p. 15, answer the following:
   a. Leadership demands action. What would be your action as a leader in this situation?
   b. Leadership means influencing others. Would you lead by example or directive? How would you like to influence the thoughts, feelings, or actions of those in your group?
   c. Leadership happens in the context of a group. Who are the people you would be working with?
   d. Leadership involves reaching a goal together. What is your goal for the group?
   e. Leadership demands that the group and the leader share a goal. How would you get the rest of your group on board with this goal?
3. Identify the specific steps you will take in the next three months to lead in this situation. Put them in your calendar and treat them as tasks to be completed.
4. If possible, evaluate your experience after three months. How well did you follow your plan? Did your group move toward or achieve its goal? How did your actions move the group forward?

Endnotes

1. Team Technology, "The Basics of Team Building . . . and the Problem with Groups," 2001, www.teamtechnology.co.uk/tt/t-articl/tb-basic.htm.
2. Alfie Cohen, *No Contest: A Case against Competition*. Boston: Houghton Mifflin, 1992.
3. John D. Mayer, Peter Salovey, and David R. Caruso, "Emotional Intelligence: New Ability or Eclectic Traits?," September 2008, *American Psychologist,* 63, no. 6, p. 503.
4. Institute for Health and Human Potential, "What is EQ?", 2011, www.ihhp.com/what_is_eq.htm.
5. Carol Carter, *Keys to Business Communication: Success in College, Career, & Life,* Upper Saddle River, NJ: Pearson Education, 2012, p. 51.
6. W. Glenn Rowe, ed, *Cases in Leadership,* 2007, www.corwin.com/upm-data/15104_Rowe_Chapter_01.pdf.
7. http://www.findthebestjobs.net/top-10-skills-employers-look-for-in-an-interview-part-I
8. http://www.likeateam.com/7-benefits-of-teamwork.html
9. http://quazen.com/kids-and-teens/school-time/teamwork-in-the-animal-kingdom/